Mighty Machines

FIRE TRUCKS
AND RESCUE VEHICLES

Jean Coppendale

FIREFLY BOOKS

A FIREFLY BOOK

Published by Firefly Books Ltd. 2010

Third printing, 2013

Publisher Cataloging-in-Publication Data (U.S.)

Coppendale, Jean.
   Fire trucks and rescue vehicles : mighty machines / Jean Coppendale.
[24] p. : col. photos. ;   cm.
Includes index.
Summary: A fun book about fire trucks and rescue vehicles for young readers, including lifeboats, rescue helicopters and motorcycle patrols.
ISBN-13: 978-1-55407-621-5 (pbk.)

1. Fire engines – Juvenile literature. I. Title.
[E] 628.9259 dc22   TH9372.C677 2010

Library and Archives Canada Cataloguing in Publication

A CIP record for this book is available from Library and Archives Canada

Published in the United States by
Firefly Books (U.S.) Inc.
P.O. Box 1338, Ellicott Station
Buffalo, New York 14205

Published in Canada by
Firefly Books Ltd.
50 Staples Avenue, Unit 1
Richmond Hill, Ontario L4B OA7

Printed in China

Author Jean Coppendale
Designer Rahul Dhiman (Q2A Media)
Editor Katie Bainbridge
Picture Researcher Jyoti Sachdev (Q2A Media)

Publisher Steve Evans
Creative Director Zeta Davies
Senior Editor Hannah Ray

Picture credits
Key: t = top, b = bottom, c = center,
l = left, r = right, FC = front cover
Keith Levit/ **Shutterstock:** 4–5; **Photo Researchers, Inc./ Photolibrary:** 5t;
Mauritius Die Bildagentur Gmbh/ **Photolibrary:** 6–7; Micah May/ **Shutterstock:** 7t;
BIOS Gunther Michel/ **Still Pictures:** 8–9; Markus Dlouhy/ **Still Pictures:** 9b;
Oshkosh Truck Corporation: 10–11; **Index Stock Imagery/ Photolibrary:** 12–13;
Photo Researchers, Inc./ Photolibrary: 13t; Mark William Penny/ **Shutterstock:** 14–15;
LA(Phot) Emma Somerfield/ Royal Navy: 15t; **Oshkosh Truck Corporation:** 16–17;
OEAMTC: 17t; **Ford Motor Company:** 18–19; Jochen Tack/ **Still Pictures:** 19t;
REUTERS/ Fabrizio Bensch: 20b; **REUTERS**/ Guido Benschop: 20–21

Manufactured by 1010 Printing International Ltd. in Huizhou, Guangdong, China in August 2011, Job #JQ11070161.

Words in **bold** can be found in the glossary on page 23.

Contents

Quick! Emergency!

If there is an accident or if someone is in trouble, an emergency **vehicle** and specially trained people rush to the scene to help.

Whenever there is a traffic accident or emergency, the police come to help out.

Fire engines, ambulances, police cars, lifeboats and rescue helicopters are all emergency vehicles. Most emergency cars and trucks have a **siren** and flashing lights. These let people know to clear the way for emergency vehicles when they are racing through traffic.

Help! Fire!

Fire engines and fire trucks arrive quickly to put out a fire. Fire engines have tanks of water with hoses that are used to pour water onto the fire. Fire trucks have long ladders that are used to rescue people from high buildings. Firefighters wear special uniforms and helmets to protect them from the smoke and the heat of the flames.

Fire trucks have metal arms at the side. This is to stop the truck from tipping over when the ladder is being used.

Fire truck ladders can be turned in all directions to reach people trapped in fires.

Forest fires

In some countries, forest fires start when the weather is very hot and dry. Special airplanes and helicopters are used to put out these fires. A tank full of water is carried underneath the airplane or helicopter. **Pilots** can open the water tank using special controls.

As this Firehawk helicopter flies over the forest, it drops water onto the fire below.

Helicopters are also used to rescue people or animals from hard-to-reach places. This is a mountain rescue helicopter carrying a dog to safety.

Airport accidents

Special equipment is needed to fight fires in airports. This is because airplanes are very big. It's also because airports and airplanes are usually filled with hundreds of people.

Airport fire trucks are built to put out a fire on an airplane and rescue any **passengers** trapped on board the plane.

This airport truck has special lights at the front to see through thick smoke.

Harbor **Firefighter**

The **harbor** in New York City is used by hundreds of people every day. If a fire starts, the New York City Fire Department has a special boat called *Firefighter* that goes to the rescue.

The boat carries extra-long hoses and big water tanks to put out fires quickly and stop them from spreading.

Fireboats can pump a lot of water onto a fire and can rescue both people and **goods**.

Other harbors have fireboats, too. They put out fires on ships and rescue passengers.

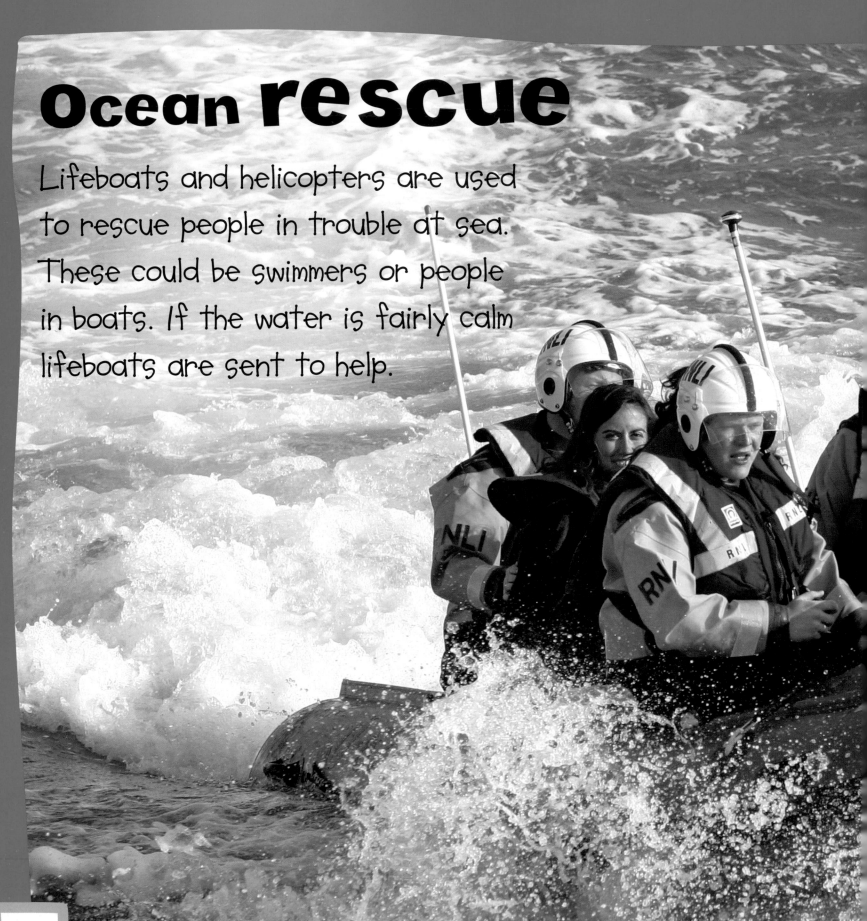

Ocean rescue

Lifeboats and helicopters are used to rescue people in trouble at sea. These could be swimmers or people in boats. If the water is fairly calm lifeboats are sent to help.

A helicopter arrives to rescue people from a sinking boat.

If the sea is very rough and it is not safe for the lifeboats, helicopters are used to **hoist** people to safety.

Send an **ambulance!**

If someone has been badly **injured** or suddenly becomes very ill, an ambulance is called. The ambulance puts on its flashing lights and loud siren and rushes to help the person, or take the person to the hospital.

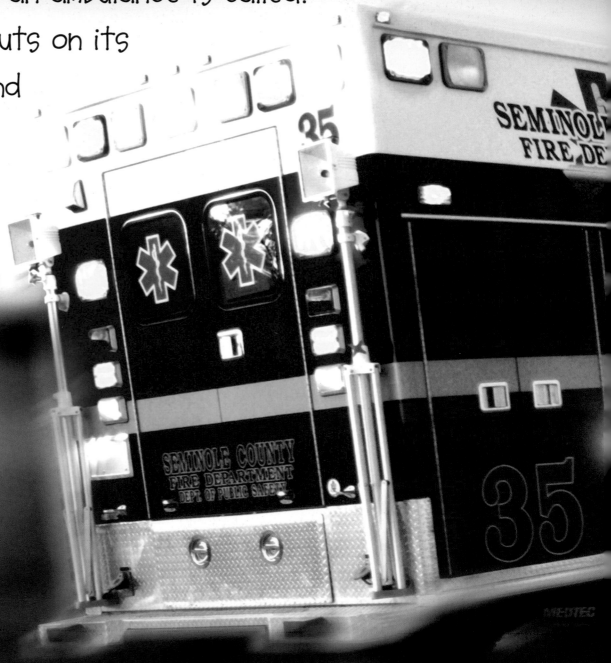

Inside the back of an ambulance is a bed, medical equipment, and somewhere for the **paramedics** to sit.

Some places are difficult to reach by road. An air ambulance helicopter is used instead.

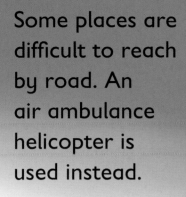

Paramedics are people trained to care for the sick or injured person inside the ambulance.

Police on the way!

Police cars can race to the scene of a crime or accident. Police drivers have been trained to drive at high speeds on busy roads and highways.

Police cars have computers that allow officers to check information, such as if a car is stolen or not.

Sometimes a police helicopter is used to chase people on the roads who are speeding, or **criminals** who are trying to escape.

Motorcycle patrol

In very crowded cities, some police use motorcycles to help them reach an accident quickly or chase criminals through busy streets.

Sometimes motorcycle police travel with the cars of important people in order to keep them safe.

Motorcycle police always wear safety helmets and they have to be specially trained to ride their bikes.

Activities

- Start your own collection of emergency vehicle pictures. Group them together — for example, ambulances, fire engines, police cars and so on. Which are your favorites? Why?

- Do you know what each of these emergency vehicles is used for? What can you see in each picture?

- On a big sheet of paper, draw your favorite emergency vehicle. Then imagine there is a telephone call. There has been an accident. Quick, you must help! Make up a story about what happens next.

- Which vehicle does a police officer drive?

Glossary

Criminals
People who have broken the law by doing something such as stealing.

Goods
Things such as clothes, food, cars or books. They can be moved by boat, plane, train or truck.

Harbor
A safe place where ships and boats can stay. This is where boats unload and collect their goods and where passenger boats pick up and drop off people.

Hoist
To pull someone on board a plane or helicopter using a rope.

Injured
When someone has been hurt.

Paramedics
The men and women who drive the ambulance and care for injured people until they reach the hospital.

Passengers
People who travel inside a car, bus, train, boat or airplane.

Pilots
The people who fly planes and helicopters.

Siren
A loud noise used by emergency vehicles when they are traveling very fast. It's used to warn other vehicles on the road that an emergency vehicle is coming through.

Vehicle
A car, truck, motorcycle or anything else that travels on the road.

Index